LOVE

"A Man's Perspective"

LOVE

"A Man's Perspective"

WRITTEN AND EDITED BY

TINA CASH

authorHOUSE®

AuthorHouse™
1663 Liberty Drive
Bloomington, IN 47403
www.authorhouse.com
Phone: 1-800-839-8640

Published by AuthorHouse   11/07/2012

ISBN: 978-1-4772-8966-2 (sc)
ISBN: 978-1-4772-8967-9 (hc)
ISBN: 978-1-4772-8968-6 (e)

Library of Congress Control Number: 2012921311

Any people depicted in stock imagery provided by Thinkstock are models, and such images are being used for illustrative purposes only.
Certain stock imagery © Thinkstock.

This book is printed on acid-free paper.

Because of the dynamic nature of the Internet, any web addresses or links contained in this book may have changed since publication and may no longer be valid. The views expressed in this work are solely those of the author and do not necessarily reflect the views of the publisher, and the publisher hereby disclaims any responsibility for them.

KJV is 100% in the public domain. All bibles have a range given by the publisher that allows a certain amount of text to be used without the need for written permission. The range can be from 250 to 500 verses allowed. Often the publishers state that the author must come up with at least 75% original content, as well, but it can go up to 95%. If the author wants to know how much text they can use then they can go to the publishing company's website and the information should be there. The bible publishers also have a set way they want their bible cited and the author will be able to find that on the web page, too.

TABLE OF CONTENTS

PREFACE

I like to thank God first for giving me the strength and courage to move forward. This book was inspired from personal experiences in my own life. I have been married, divorced, met a few good men, some bad ones, and a few in between. After years of my experiences, I was curious to find out men's perspective on love.

While I am a woman and usually I think with my heart, I desired insight as to the thoughts of men from different arenas of life. As women we first look to the men in our lives as role models, these men include our fathers, grandfathers, uncles or whoever was placed in your life. Women (not all) have the tendency to look for that image in a man, or the opposite of your role model. My role model was my grandfather, we called him granddaddy Baker. Granddaddy Baker was a hard-working man, married my grandmother, Ella Baker who had five children previously to marrying granddaddy. Although not one child was granddaddy Baker's, no one would have known that. He helped my grandmother raise them, financially support them and her, and helped all of his grandchildren to include myself. I saw agape love through my grandparents. My grandmother was a wise woman who opened her home to everyone and always let my grandfather know what he meant to her. My grandmother was beautiful, while my grandfather was not the most attractive gentleman. Yet he was just that, a gentleman. She was his queen and he was her king. We seldom saw them argue. They helped each other in the kitchen, around the house, in the yard, financially and spiritually. They weren't perfect, but perfect love covers all imperfections. That was imparted in me. Love is not perfect, but you should be willing to work through each other's imperfections.

If you don't have any positive role models in your family, look to people who are close to you, who have been married for quite some time.

"Love a Man's Perspective" is truly Love God's Preferred Way. Man's perspective can be tainted by hurts, pains, and bad experiences. In the interim we exclude the most important part of love, "God". God's love covers a multitude of sin. It's forgiving, never holding a grudge, leaves the past in the past, but presses on to the future.

I have in the past look for love in the wrong places and people. You and I together will seek what we really need. While hearing from men giving insight as to the desires of a man's heart.

I would like to also thank my mother Gail Harris, who told me to believe in the impossible and that I could do anything I put my mind to. Thanks to my father John Harris who helped to give me life and imparted never to settle for less. Thanks to my three sons for bearing with me through this project, Derrick, Devon and Dontre Cash. Thanks also to my spiritual mothers in the Lord, Apostle Lois Parchment and Eloise Johnson. I would also like to thank my siblings, Tonya Harris and John Harris and their children Tiona and Waymon Bryd, Lakisha and Joe Claxton (and Children), and Kashawn Harris.

Thanks to several dear friends who listened, stood by me during the good, the bad, divorce, bad relationships, love, and just because: Marcia Miller who was a personal muse, Pastor Fern Boone, Margarita Henry, and Robin Bridgewater. I like to thank an attorney who helped me with some legality's and wanted to remain anonymous. I thank all the participants of this book. I like to thank all of my personal relationships that pushed me to inquire and desire to know a man's perspective on love.

INTRODUCTION

We go through life with sayings such as: "Women are from Venus—Men are from Mars"; "A Man or Women is Complex"; "True Love is Hard to Find". As these are just sayings, they also pierce the heart of many; leaving men and women, with a feeling of truth to the sayings. Last but not least, the infamous saying "What's love got to do with it?"

Actually, love has everything to do with it. Men and women alike, desire love from that special someone. They desire what the world considers a soul mate, someone to spend a lifetime with. While looking for that soul mate, you should ask yourself; what is it that you are truly looking for? Woman, are you looking for a knight in shining armor, a Donald Trump or Morris Chestnut; and men are you looking for a Halle Berry or a Beyonce? Are you looking for a certain image, a fixation of your imaginary desires; or a person you can relate, communicate and have similar values?

Some women equate love to the Karats that a man places on her finger, or if the man is financially established and able to satisfy the woman's desires materially. Some women equate love with the man verbally acknowledging he loves her, but exemplifies no actions to validate the statement.

Men can misconceive lust for love. If a woman satisfies a man's desire sexually, then he may misinterpret the lust fulfillment for love fulfillment. A man or woman may also turn a physical attraction, meaning the man or woman is physically attractive in a pleasing manner, to what they consider love. Physical attraction differentiates with each individual. In the same respect love is defined by each individual, and there is no true and finite meaning of love. Each person has their personal definition of what they assume love is. Webster dictionary's definition of love is: a (1): strong affection for another arising out of kinship or personal ties <maternal love for a child> (2): attraction based on sexual desire: affection and tenderness felt by lovers (3): affection based on admiration, benevolence, or common interests <love for his old schoolmates>, etc.

LOVE, to me is unexplainable, heartfelt, emotional, sincere, true to who you are; unpredictable, a vast array of winds flowing from one end of the earth to another, a sunset sky, the glistening of the noon day on the ocean, a waterfall, the mountains with snow covered tips, the smell of the dew in the morning, a field of pansies; a cup of hot chocolate with whip cream and marsh-mellows, your favorite dessert, a walk through the park, an Olympian winning a gold medal; the basketball, football, or soccer team winning the championship; the first touch of a newborn infant; every first thereafter, desirable, all of God's creation and God himself; what you choose to make it, LOVE. What's your perspective?

I am not promising to help you receive, a companion, friend, soul mate, husband or wife. What you will receive are different views on love. This book is a conglomeration of interviews, several men and their outlook about love.

In today's society women and men have created an ideology of what love looks like and what love is. Defining love and writing a list of their requirements for a mate. I ask you to put the pen and paper away from the list, and just maybe you and I can form a new or tangible idea about love after reading the insights and stories of these men. Each and every participant in the book is a real person and not fictitious. If you are a man, you may be able to relate to these men and their synopsis. If you are a woman, you will get one on one insight into how men from all facets of life and varied age groups view women and love.

PASSION

Cedric Campbell is a Producer, Videographer, Film Maker, Actor, and Play-wright. He is a forty-two year old single man who resembles Denzel Washington.

Cedric states: I feel love is a common bond between two people who share the same or similar values of the other person. I have been in love before, but the love that I desire entails mutual understanding between my-self and my partner. My desire is a friendship that goes along with the idea of sharing commonalities and views. Not in a big way, in a simple way. Where there is always room for love to grow stronger.

Through my love hurts, I've learned not to be naive and to keep an open mind in my relationships. I allow myself to cope with the possibility that something may go wrong. Although, I am trying to stay optimistic, I'm leaving room for that maybe. Insecurity is not one of my character traits, nor am I egocentric.

I have met women who do not appreciate the small things. When the simple things are not appreciated, for me, I get bored and tend to want out of the relationship. I don't believe in playing elementary games. I'm either in or out. There comes a point in life where you have to grow up. I can't govern anyone else actions, only my own. There are times that you screw up in relationships, say the wrong thing, miscommunicate, or just don't know how to satisfy your partner. I can't be that fictitious dream that women look for. I'm going to have flaws.

Even with those flaws, like most men, I want to satisfy my partner. Sex and love are both important variables in a relationship. When you are just in a relationship for the thrills it is altogether different than when you are in love. When you are in love there is a completion. When the love and sex is combined it is better than any peppermint patty that I ever had.

Abstinence is the biblical way until marriage, but it is a problem for men and women. Although, I believe it is attainable if one desires. Society has tainted the hearts of men and women alike with visual acceptance of sex outside of marriage. Placing provocative scenes on television, and yes sex sells. Sex sells cars, liquor, lingerie and the list goes on.

Society also covers up the real meat of a relationship with material things. These material things consist of big rings, expensive gifts as priorities over men and women being in love. The everyday true life of the average person is hard working, vast responsibilities, bills, career—if not focused and balanced these could get in the way of what could be a good relationship. The choice is left to us to decide what's best. In the scheme of life, it can become messy, ad pressure if you are trying to live life happily married. Old people say "as time passes, love will cover the pressures of this world".

The question I ask: is do you as an individual embrace what life has to offer? Being rich or having material possession is not the answer. The money may only help with some of the relationship issues. I also ponder: what each person is expecting from the other? Why are you involved in the relationship? Are you truly in love? Or do you want the relationship because the person looks good, feels good or just a family tradition that you have to get married by a certain age? I don't believe you can truly be in love until you know spiritually who you are.

When you know who you are and that Christ lives in you; you will wait on God to send you a mate. Although I see nothing wrong with a woman flirting; this would help open up the dialog.

Starting a relationship is a give and take. When men go outside the relationship they are just taking. Some men cheat just to see if they can get away with it. The suspense of not being caught, it's like owning more than one car. You can pick and choose, giving a man a feeling of power. Some men feel it's advantageous to have more than one woman. It's a falsity of his imagination. Sometimes the act of infidelity has nothing to do with temptation. Having multiple partners make some men feel successful. What I call the MPS syndrome; Money, Power, and Sex. Dismissing what is truly important, Love.

Yes, love should equate to marriage. Not just sex, multiple partners or going outside your marriage. I look forward to a love that I can share, moments spent sitting by the ocean, eating strawberries, talking about life plans, simplicity; it doesn't take an air wave party; it's where life becomes serial in a sense. In my mind, *you* are the moment; whatever is going on outside of us doesn't matter.

PASSION

THOUGHT NUGGETS

But if they cannot control themselves, they should marry, for it is better to marry than to burn with passion. (1 Cor. 7:9 (NIV))

"Sexual pressure is not the best motive for getting married but it is better to marry the *right person* than to "burn with passion".

Consult God if you are in a relationship and dealing with sexual pressure due to the passion that you feel for each other. Ask God for his wisdom and staying power to remain abstinent. Although many may think abstinence is not thought of in this day. Abstinence is actually practiced more now than ever, not only due to moral conviction, but also due to the rise of sexually transmitted disease.

Seek God as in Proverbs 8:17: "I love them that love me; and these that seek me early shall find me." While seeking the love of another—God speaks and tells you to love wisdom, and if you seek it you shall find it. With wisdom comes understanding and the knowledge to know what you to look for in a mate. Love Gods wisdom and he will give it to you.

AMBITION

A young twenty-one year old Truck Driver, Ryan Miller is single but in a relationship. Ryan believes love is undefinable. He replies: Love is just a feeling, causing the bonds to meet. I can't stop thinking about the person; there is a certain feeling in your body, a quiver. It feels as if you are compatible, a reflection of who I am.

I believe you can have this feeling for more than one person in a lifetime; however it will never fell the same as the first time. I have loved with my whole heart, and I have also said I loved but didn't mean it. As a young man it was sex without loving the person. I processed my brain to believe if I don't fall in love, I wouldn't be set up for failure, hurt or pain. I lived life just fulfilling moments and the lust of my flesh.

No ties or commitment; me going my way and them going theirs. As I have gotten older, I have learned differently.

Although I feel sex is at least sixty-five percent of importance in a relationship, it is not as important with the absence of love.

We have allowed society to place its values on us. Young people fill mature by performing the act of sex. Not realizing the consequences. Not knowing the true meaning of love, how to find it, or what it looks like. The non-realization of love has caused teen age pregnancy, singles raising two and three children by themselves, and a high divorce rate. People view sex as a hobby alienating love.

I believe faith in God or whatever you consider your higher power; will direct you to the perfect person for you. I personally prefer women who take charge and are a little aggressive. However an overly aggressive woman is a turn off. Men are made to be more dominant, but I support women rights, and that a woman has the right to voice her opinion. An opinion however is just that, if the man is the head of the household, the woman should allow him to perform as the head. Leaving final decision making to him and trusting what he decides is correct. This may sound a little male chauvinistic; however, some women say they want someone with a take charge attitude, knowing what should be accomplished. When given what they ask for, problems arise when things don't go their way.

If I love you, allow me to pursue you and ask to marry you. Love will eventually turn into marriage; if I am not pressured, coerced, or manipulated into marrying. I don't want to spend the rest of my life looking for that special someone. When you find love, you will know. Don't allow it to slip away.

I was in a relationship with a person (to remain nameless); that I dearly loved. They did not see, understand or receive the love. I put the person before God, family, and probably even myself. I learned she was not the person I thought she was. After this experience, I now look for other qualities in a person other than physical appearance. Are they caring, a motivator and a true help-mate? Although I know to look deeper, my preferences are short women, outgoing, ambitious, truthful, loyal and outspoken. It truly turns me off when a woman is a nagger, clingy or a snooper (loves to investigate).

Unmarried, I am in pursuit of unconditional love. If you find true love, stay with it, know it's the correct love (not infatuation or lust); before making any decision. My advice is to take your time and don't be in a rush, love will come to you!!

AMBITION

THOUGHT NUGGETS

If you have any encouragement from being united with Christ, if any comfort from his love, if any fellowship with the spirit, if any tenderness and compassion, [2]then make my joy complete by being likeminded, having the same love, being one in spirit and purpose. [3]Do nothing out of selfish ambition or vain conceit, but in humility consider others better than your selves. [4]Each of you should look not only to your own interest, but also to the interest of others. (Phil. 2:1)

Ryan's love for his partner was unselfish in his eyes, giving all. Although Ryan was hurt, God does not want us to have selfish love as stated in Phil 2:1. God's love for us was unselfish, as he gave his only begotten son for our sins. A friend loveth at all times, and a brother is born for adversity. (Prov. 17:17)

There is no difficulty that enough love will not conquer;

no disease that enough love will not heal;

no door that enough love will not open;

no gulf that enough love will not bridge;

no wall that enough love will not throw down;

no sin that enough love will not redeem . . .

It makes no difference how deeply seated may be the

trouble;

How hopeless the outlook; how muddled the tangle; how

great the mistake.

A sufficient realization of love will dissolve it all.

Emmet Fox

(July 30, 1886-August13, 1951)

CREATE

Larry McKinzie is a fifty-five year old Juvenile Detention Officer and Poet. Mr. McKinzie is married to a beautiful woman named Deborah. They wed twenty years ago and are still going strong.

Mr. McKinzie and Deborah were high school sweethearts. He left to go to the military and was stationed in Germany. During that time Mr. Mckinzie said; Deborah wrote while I was away, one day a specific letter came and a light bulb went off, I knew at that point she was the one. I wrote her every day for the next fourteen days in a row. I proposed and of course she couldn't turn me down, and said yes. There was something special about this woman. As time went on and

I returned home from the military we became husband and wife.

I found a love. She can read my mind and I can read hers. We finish each other's sentences. We know the dos and don'ts of each other, not to cross the line, giving the respect due to one another. We became one.

Love is deeper than just sex. Most people think love and sex are the same. Once they perform the act of sex they assume they are in love. Love is lasting. Sex is fleeting. Love is selflessness. Sex is self-gratification. Animals have the instinct to have sex with no feelings. Humans consider this action as animalistic behavior. However, some humans also have the ability to have sex with no feelings, although we were created to have thoughts and feelings which can evolve into love, not just the act of sex.

I love Deborah as an individual, her mind, thoughtfulness and caring attitude. Deborah initially was the pursuer of the relationship. I was a little taken back, but it was not a turn off for me. I realized she knew what she wanted, and I fell deeply in love as she was what I wanted as well. I'm not suggesting that women should go and pursue after men. This was our circumstance and it worked out well.

I have a saying, that there a four things that women need. A woman needs a Jaguar in her garage, a mink in her closet, a tiger in the bed, a jack-ass to pay for it all, and a seal—to seal the deal.

CREATE

THOUGHT NUGGETS

⁷I form the light, and create darkness, I make peace, and create evil; I the Lord do all these things.

⁸Drop down, ye heavens, from above and let the skies pour down righteousness; let the earth open, and let them bring forth salvation, and let righteousness spring up together; I the Lord created it. (Isaiah 45:7-8)

God created all of the above. He also has your mate created exactly for you. Be still and wait on him. The Lord God handles all things. Allow him to handle this area of your life.

Love never gives up.

Love cares more for others than for self.

Love doesn't want what it doesn't have.

Love doesn't strut,

Doesn't have a swelled head,

Doesn't force itself on others,

Isn't always "me first,"

Doesn't fly off the handle,

Doesn't keep score of the sins of others,

Doesn't revel when others grovel,

Takes pleasure in the flowering of truth,

Puts up with anything,

Trusts God always

Always looks for the best,

Never looks back

But keeps going to the end.

(1 Cor. 13:3-7)

PROTECTOR

Thirty-four year old Sherman Delva is a Detention Officer and Preacher; divorcee with three wonderful children. Sherman believes that respect is the most important attribute of love. Sherman expounds: if a woman loves a man she would do everything in her power to understand him. We live in a world where the whole world is on the man's shoulders and we can come home frustrated. In the African American culture sometimes the man takes his frustration out on his wife, not intentionally, but because of the stress. African American women take it personal and lash back at the man. The woman is not understanding of the man's hard day at work and the stress the man is under. I believe that a woman should understand and deal with everyday issues that may incur. Love is understanding, putting up with your spouse when they are not loveable, respecting and not embarrassing your spouse in front of people, not exposing the skeletons in your closets, covering and acknowledging each other even when undeserved. Love is putting up with each other's baggage, and being submissive as the woman.

My favorite quote of love is: "It is impossible to fall out of love, love is such a powerful emotion that once it involves you it does not depart, true love is eternal, if you think you were once in love, but fell out of it, than it wasn't love you were in. There are no exit signs in love; there is only an on ramp" (Author unknown). My take on how you know when you are in love is, even when your significant other gains weight, it wouldn't matter. You want to protect and be there for her if anything bad happens in her life. You don't hold grudges, release and forgive. You don't allow your emotions to control your actions. When things go sour or you have disagreements, you don't try and look for another woman or go outside of your commitment. You stay and work on the relationship.

If you love someone you don't intentionally hurt them. You don't play with emotions.

If you are not married you should not partake in sexual conduct. Sex is physical but also an emotional attachment. It should be a part of love but not love itself. Sex is important but also dangerous. If not married, one individual could perform the act for only physical pleasure, while the other person is emotionally attached. This leads to hurt and pain on one party or the other. When having sex you are giving of yourself, while the sex is temporal, love is eternal. If I give of me, I want the eternal love.

People in general abuse the word Love. As song writer Kirk Franklin said: "Love a word that comes to me but few people really knows what it means to love somebody." Another song writer wrote: "love so many people use your name in vain." I believe people abuse love because they don't understand it.

As a preacher I don't see religion as love. There are so many types of religion. I do believe that Christianity and love intertwine. As a Christian you should show the love of God to all those that you come in contact. This should include your spouse, fiancé, or girlfriend. If you are not married, I think the man should pursue the woman. Women, yes your outer appearance is important. A man cannot initially see your spirit or your soul. Men are visual beings, we pay attention to a woman's hair, feet and nails; and if she is well groomed and attractive. That is the natural side of a man, after we see what we like, we then look deeper for other characteristics. I prefer a woman that is not deceptive, very genuine, someone I can call a friend, and submissive. It is a total turn off if a woman is a liar has wrong motives, a bad attitude, arrogant, and prideful.

When I love, I love hard, not looking at the money a woman makes, or what she can bring to the table. Love goes beyond income or economic status. I love the person for who they are. The divorce rate has escalated due to misguided expectations. The wedding vows usually say, for better or for worse, for richer or for poorer, till death do us part. If we truly love, we would keep those vows. Jesus said "if you love me, you would keep my commandments". So I think we should relate that statement in every part of our lives, not breaking promises or commitments. When couples get married they focus so much on the wedding, investing thousands of dollars on the event. Instead of investing on the actual event, they should invest in the relationship to maintain the marriage and not end up in divorce.

Although I am a divorcee, I do not agree with divorce. I am looking forward to marriage again, and in my new wife the qualities I would like to find include a woman that loves God first. If she loves God, then she will accept God's guidance on how to love me.

PROTECTOR

THOUGHT NUGGETS

> Psalm 59:9—O my Strength, I will watch *and* give
> heed to you *and* sing praises, for God is my Defense
> (my Protector and High Tower).

Women and men have the assurance that God will watch over you. He will protect you from the counterfeit, imitator, perpetrator, and those who are not for your best interest. He is the strength you need to hold on until that right person is sent your way. Praise God ahead of time for his strength and protection.

Pastor Sherman describes the love he desires, he describes that the women will love God. If she loves God she should possess the fruit of the spirit. The fruit of the spirit [holy spirit] which can only be given by God is described in Galatians 5:22-23 (Amplified Bible)—22But the fruit of the [Holy] Spirit [the work which His presence within accomplishes] is love, joy (gladness), peace, patience (an even temper, forbearance), kindness, goodness (benevolence), faithfulness, [23]Gentleness (meekness, humility), self-control (self-restraining, continence). Against such things there is no law.

SUSTAIN

Willie Johnson is a husband of forty-one years, a father of two adult children and a proud grandfather. Love, Mr. Johnson says is companionship with each other. When you have someone you love, it's what you do with your emotions for the rest of your marriage. How do you forgive when situations arise? Little issues come up and people want out immediately asking for a divorce. True love fights through the issues and situations. You need to be able to forgive and let go. No one in any marriage is perfect. The best part of breaking up is making up. When making up don't misconceive that the sex solves the problem. It doesn't, communications solves problems. Don't mistake lust for love. Love is durability, being able to bounce back from every circumstance. Some will say that they are in love, when it's only words. Words are cheap, durability you know why you are there. You are in it for the long haul.

There are different types of love. There is affectionate love, where one may like to show how they feel towards the other. That may be your touchy, feely couple. There is nothing wrong with that, if that's what you like. There is the companionship love, where you all are talkers and share your emotions with one another. I think both combined is a good formula for a lasting love.

Men sometimes do not play an emotional part in a relationship. But it is important, for a man to let a woman know that she is loved in a marriage. If the man is not married, most men will say anything, even I love you if that's what the woman needs to hear in order to get what he wants. There is a quote in the bible that says it is better to marry than to burn. But why would you, if you don't have to.

I remember in my time, you use to go on several dates and get to know each other. Now they sleep with each other the first night they meet. This leaves nothing special to look forward too. The mystery is gone; it's been laid on the table before you. If you marry someone after not getting to know that person, and you slept together quickly, how would you truly trust that person? If she/he was that easy, what else would they do?

Once married, the biggest mistake people make is trying to change a person. You can't make someone into something you want them to be. If you take the time to get to know them, then you will have an idea of the type of person you are marrying. This doesn't mean that either party will not get tempted. Temptation is always waiting around the corner. I was working out one day, minding my own business. A young woman was exercising on the treadmill next to me. All of a sudden I see her bending over showing all of her rear end along with her thong. I thought temptation knocking at my door. I said, **RUN** Willy **RUN**, and did just that. After forty-one years of marriage, no temptation is worth losing my wife.

Women, if you truly desire a husband, not a boyfriend, boy toy, or whatever you call it in these days. Don't show all your goods. Give the man a chance to pursue you. Men don't like rejection, so if you have to, let him down easily. If he truly wants you, he will continue to chase you. I don't agree with internet dating, strictly because where is the real pursuit or romance. It's a fantasy because the woman or men believes everything the other side is saying. They have no evidence of where the person truly lives, if he/she is actually who they say they are, and no one on one contact. You can tell quite a bit from someone's eyes, smile, and gestures. I'm not saying there are no exceptions to this, as there are always exceptions to everything. But on the average you need personal communication, via dating or phone.

My marriage has lasted this long because I looked for a woman who I could trust. She was and is a well dresser. She is a lady in and outside of our home. She is respected by others, my-self and our children. She has helped me to strive for better days, better jobs, and to be a better man. She is truly my better half and help mate. I pray I am what she needs as well.

SUSTAIN

THOUGHT NUGGETS

Song of Solomon 2
Amplified Bible (AMP)

2 [She said] I am only a little rose *or* autumn crocus of the plain of Sharon, or a [humble] lily of the valleys [that grows in deep and difficult places].

² But Solomon replied, Like the lily among thorns, so are you, my love, among the daughters.

³ Like an apple tree among the trees of the wood, so is my beloved [shepherd] among the sons [cried the girl]! Under his shadow I delighted to sit, and his fruit was sweet to my taste.

⁴ He brought me to the banqueting house, and his banner over me was love [for love waved as a

protecting and comforting banner over my head when I was near him].

⁵ Sustain me with raisins, refresh me with apples, for I am sick with love.

⁶ [I can feel] [a]his left hand under my head and his right hand embraces me!

⁷ [He said] I charge you, O you daughters of Jerusalem, by the gazelles or by the hinds of the field [which are free to follow their own instincts] that you not try to stir up or awaken [my] love until it pleases.

⁸ [Vividly she pictured it] The voice of my beloved [shepherd]! Behold, he comes, leaping upon the mountains, bounding over the hills.

⁹ My beloved is like a gazelle or a young hart. Behold, he stands behind the wall of our house, he

looks in through the windows, he glances through the lattice.

[10] My beloved speaks and says to me, Rise up, my love, my fair one, and come away.

[11] For, behold, the winter is past; the rain is over and gone.

[12] The flowers appear on the earth; the time of the singing [of birds] has come, and the voice of the turtledove is heard in our land.

[13] The fig tree puts forth *and* ripens her green figs, and the vines are in blossom and give forth their fragrance. [b]Arise, my love, my fair one, and come away.

[14] [So I went with him, and when we were climbing the rocky steps up the hillside, my beloved shepherd said to me] O my dove, [while you are here] in the seclusion of the clefts in the solid rock, in the

sheltered *and* secret place of the cliff, let me see your face, [c]let me hear your voice; for your voice is sweet, and your face is lovely.

15 [My heart was touched and I fervently sang to him my desire] Take for us the foxes, the [d]little foxes that spoil the vineyards [of our love], for our vineyards are in blossom.

16 [She said distinctly] My beloved is mine and I am his! He pastures his flocks among the lilies.

17 [Then, longingly addressing her absent shepherd, she cried] Until the day breaks and the shadows flee away, return hastily, O my beloved, and be like a gazelle or a young hart as you cover the mountains [which separate us].

SUSTAINING is a hard gesture. We live in a quick and fast world. Fast food, fast cars, quick technology, we want everything fast and as Burger King motto state: "Have it your way". We also want it our way. But in order to sustain, you may have to give and take, bend a little, give of your-self a little. It is worth sustaining, if you can find a love like Solomon. Solomon was sick with love. He loved whole heartedly. Is this appealing to you?

LEAD

Apostle, Senior Pastor, soon to be Husband, father and entrepreneur Kevin Robinson; forty-eight year old man of God was more than willing to share his views on Love.

Apostle Robinson believes love is sharing, honoring, commitment, being on one accord, and adoring the opposite sex. He states: I have never truly been in love before until now. I thought I was, but in actuality it wasn't. I fell in love, with the idea of being in love; I was infatuated but not really in love. We had a few things in common. True love does not hurt, disrespect, operate in rejection, and love does not harm, and that is what I felt in my past relationships.

I know when I'm in love because of the things that I look for in a woman. My heart feels and beats a certain way for her. It's like a person having a sponge; I can feel her, and believe she can feel me. A sponge draws water, my fiancé draws me in. The first time I saw her I knew she was my wife. It was something that connected. I knew that was her, she was the one, our spirits connected. Sometimes you can see people through lust, this wasn't that. I told a friend I was about to get married, God mad a divine connection.

There are different variations of love; I can't share the love I have for one woman with everyone. I love hard; you don't spread that with anyone.

Sex is a very important part of love; I can say I love sex. I believe when you love a person; intimacy wise you can give your all, there should not be any limitations. When I was not saved, it was just sex, it was not love making. When you're in love with an individual it would be more intimacy. You can feel their heart beat, the two people become one. When you're not in love, there is no feeling, rules or commitment. When you look through the microscope and examine the true particles of sex and love, that minute molecule of sex will make the freak come out of you. You want to please that individual.

All the molecules form together and create true love making.

Men like to pursue women because we are naturally hunters, and a woman is a lamb. I believe God is love. If the lamb (woman) knows God and loves God, you wouldn't have a problem loving the individual. If you love God, you would not also cheat on God. Men should also know how to treat God's daughter. Men cheat because some men feel sexually unsatisfied. There is no excuse for going outside the compounds of a marriage. If not married and you are engaged, in order to hold on. I believe, if you love the individual, why wait a year or longer, if it is true love. Some people feel you haven't gotten to know the person in that short period of time. I look at it the same way God does, he loves us in spite of our background, the way the person is. God will do the changing. Allow him.

As I stated before, I met my fiancée Marcia and I knew immediately that she was my wife. She showed me that she cared, we shared special days and activities. It was the small things. She was a Christian woman, but not an old fuddy dud—trying to be so religious where we could not enjoy ourselves. God is not boring. I could not handle a woman who was a complainer, didn't dress nicely, and did not love God.

My fiancé Marcia makes me laugh, even when the jokes are corny. She is adventurous and sexy. Her confidence won me over. She smelled good and every time I saw her she looked exquisite. Her voice melts my spirit. I can't go a day without talking to her. She is my fix.

LEAD

THOUGHT NUGGETS

Exodus 15:13

New International Version (NIV)

> ¹³ In your unfailing love you will lead
> the people you have redeemed.
> In your strength you will guide them
> to your holy dwelling.

Allow God to lead your steps in finding the love you look for. He has redeemed you for a time as this. When you allow God, not you, he will guide you in the right direction. He will give you the strength you need on your journey of love.

Proverbs 31:10-31

New International Version (NIV)

Epilogue: The Wife of Noble Character

10 [b]A wife of noble character who can find?

She is worth far more than rubies.

11 Her husband has full confidence in her

and lacks nothing of value.

12 She brings him good, not harm,

all the days of her life.

13 She selects wool and flax

and works with eager hands.

14 She is like the merchant ships,

bringing her food from afar.

15 She gets up while it is still night;

she provides food for her family

and portions for her female servants.

16 She considers a field and buys it;

out of her earnings she plants a vineyard.

¹⁷ She sets about her work vigorously;

her arms are strong for her tasks.

¹⁸ She sees that her trading is profitable,

and her lamp does not go out at night.

¹⁹ In her hand she holds the distaff

and grasps the spindle with her fingers.

²⁰ She opens her arms to the poor

and extends her hands to the needy.

²¹ When it snows, she has no fear for her
household;

for all of them are clothed in scarlet.

²² She makes coverings for her bed;

she is clothed in fine linen and purple.

²³ Her husband is respected at the city gate,

where he takes his seat among the elders of the
land.

²⁴ She makes linen garments and sells them,

and supplies the merchants with sashes.

²⁵ She is clothed with strength and dignity;

she can laugh at the days to come.

²⁶ She speaks with wisdom,

and faithful instruction is on her tongue.

²⁷ She watches over the affairs of her household

and does not eat the bread of idleness.

²⁸ Her children arise and call her blessed;

her husband also, and he praises her:

²⁹ "Many women do noble things,

but you surpass them all."

³⁰ Charm is deceptive, and beauty is fleeting;

but a woman who fears the Lord is to be praised.

[31] Honor her for all that her hands have done,

and let her works bring her praise at the city gate.

The Proverbs 31 woman is what most Christian men and non-Christian men desire in a wife. Apostle Robinson found his Proverb 31 women in his fiancé Marcia. Can you say that you are a Proverb 31 woman?

PROVIDER

Some men prefer discreetness, and I respect their wishes. With that said, the next man's perspective is from a man who is an independent Financial Advisor who would like to keep his name incognito. We will refer to him as Broker Man. Broker Man is fifty-one years old, divorced father of four children, three boys and one girl. Ladies just some information between you and I—Mr. Broker Man is also quite the looker.

Let's take a stroll down Wall Street and see what the stocks look like to Broker Man. Broker Man confides: as a Financial Advisor I deal with various investments on a daily basis. Love is an investment. You invest your time, energy and money. I honestly cannot say if I have found love. The definitive definition is not the same as my personal definition. As for me, it is a feeling of joy when you meet or see the person, a longing to be with the person; someone you want to share time and life experiences with. You expect that they are your best friend, will take the good with the bad; your companion. Whether financially stable or not, they are in it with you. To me that's unconditional love. The person you really want to spend the rest of your life with.

At present I am not sure as of yet if it is the buzz word "love" that I am feeling. I am dating someone and feeling pretty good, but I don't know if it's a rebound relationship, it's too early to know. I know I enjoy spending time with her. She is classy, intelligent and seems to have herself together. I like a confident woman.

Most women question whether their man is faithful or not. To me that shows insecurity, not confidence. Faithfulness in my opinion is not about cheating or not cheating. Men have animalistic instincts, men chase women, sometimes vice versa. In the old days men had many wives, the only rule of thumb was the man had to be able to provide.

Recognizing it is a different world, and we live in different times, not that long ago the man was the head of his household. I believe we need some of those old values back. My parents were married fifty-five years, my father was the *man* and my mother was the *woman.* He was the provider and she took care of the household responsibilities. I realize it's harder in the world today. The economy requires a two income household, if the husband cannot afford to take full responsibility for all of the household bills. People are also changing. Women sometimes present themselves in a way that is not to be respected; meaning how a woman dresses, how she carries herself, the way she speaks—give men an ideal of what type of woman she is. If she dresses provocatively, is loud and unruly, most men tend to loose respect.

If a woman is respected, men would not look at her for sex only. Although sex is critical in any relationship. If the sex isn't good, it isn't going to work. Sex is beautiful and natural between a male and a female. Sex is even better when married. It's human nature when you take the oath of marriage to desire your partner. When you go outside of the marriage—you break that marriage vow. Although society tells us that we are supposed to remain monogamous, it is not natural for a man to be with one woman. That is the reason so many good men fall. Women do a better job being monogamous. It's the woman's own mindset of how the world views them. Society doesn't view women in a positive light if they have multiple sex partners. Men are given a break. We get away with it a little more, and women are more likely to forgive men for their indiscretions. Men have a tendency not to forgive women and end relationships.

A man nor a woman should allow society to dictate the way they choose to live. It should be up to the individual to have enough self-esteem to determine their own lifestyle. A woman's self-esteem also relates to how she feels about her outward appearance. Beauty is in the eye of the beholder. So women behold your own beauty. Know that you are beautiful without a man telling you so. If you are secure within yourself, you would not have to approach the man. However, I find it a turn on for a woman to pursue a man in a tasteful manner. A little hint here or there, a smile, then allow me to make the move.

I would not marry a woman who is to forward. I believe in the institution of marriage and would definitely marry again. My natural instinct is to come home. A part of me is a player, I do it for the joy and kicks; but when it's all said and done, there is nothing like having someone to go home to.

I was married once, three or four of my previous relationships could have led to marriage. I enjoyed my life and have no regrets. I have never tried to screw over or hurt a woman. I believe in being transparent, no lies. The "truth" is the best remedy when it comes to love.

PROVIDER

THOUGHT NUGGET

Matthew 6:11-13

(New King James Version)

[11]Give us today our daily bread

[12]Forgive us our debts,

As we forgive our debtors.

[13]And lead us not into temptation,

But deliver us from the evil one.

Bible Commentary:

6:11-13 When we pray Give us today our daily bread," we are acknowledging that God is our sustainer and provider. It is a misconception to think that we provide for our needs ourselves. We must trust God daily to provide what he knows we need.

While you are praying or asking God for your husband or your wife for financial reasons, loneliness, or temptation. Allow God to be the provider in your life. In due season God will send him or her in the natural.

Lots of people

Want to ride with you in the limo, but what you want

Is someone who will

Take the bus with you when the limo breaks down.

Oprah Winfrey

(born January 29, 1954)

American television host, media mogul, and philanthropist.

DESIRES

My conversation with Parrish Miller known as "PJ" was quite different; he is a twenty-seven year old producer. PJ is a single man, has never been married and has a beautiful daughter named Siria. PJ has an interesting philosophy on love.

PJ feels that God who people say is love is the biggest misconception and biggest lie. Although true love is God, it is not the way most people perceive. God can be whatever we make it. Love is also the most misunderstood emotion of all, yet the most powerful. PJ proceeded, I thought I was in love, although now I feel love is not real. I believe I was infatuated. I began to like the person a lot, and began to become a slave to that person. I don't believe that true love exist.

Even though I *love* sex, love and sex are two different emotions. Sex is just sex, if you have someone you can openly express yourself with physically, you are ahead of the game. Some people have a moral conscious and confuse sex with morality. Sex to me is like brushing your teeth, everybody does it. Women tend to be emotional creatures, until men lie to them and hurt them. Once most women are hurt they become cold. Instead of men lying to get what they want, men should tell the truth, don't tell a woman you love her just to have sex.

At the end of the day, why do we need each other if it wasn't for the physical? We all just use each other for what we want, if we couldn't get what we wanted from each other, there would be no need for the opposite sex. It's a vicious cycle of people hurting people. Women hurt men, men hurt women and then it repeats itself. The only exception that I see are those who hold religious values. Although I believe religion is slavery—and not of God—Love is free.

Although love is free, we live in a time that women are bold. Love is free, but a woman should not be so free. It is a turn off for a woman to pursue me. If she is bold enough to approach me, how many other men is she approaching. She is definitely not girlfriend or wife material. My thoughts on marriage are—many people make marriage commitments, spend about ten thousand dollars on a wedding because most women want the glitter—it's another form of slavery.

You also can't be a sheep around a bunch of wolves. I feel marriage is not necessary because we were not meant to stay with one person. Wolves tend to stay in a pack and the most dominating of the wolves gets the female wolf he desires. Men are similar. When a man gets the women he desires, you make a commitment and the women gets complacent, she doesn't do the things she use to do. Such as keeping herself up, and fulfilling the man's sexual desires. The men then feels that she is cheating, because if she is not fulfilling you, then who is she fulfilling. That feeling of betrayal is traumatizing if you are innocent in the situation, but if you yourself have dirt then it's doesn't feel as bad. The feeling of betrayal is one of the reasons men cheat. Men also cheat because women cannot handle the truth. A woman does not want to hear that the relationship is strictly physical, as the women is emotionally involved the minute that you have sex with her. After having sex, I don't have to speak or see the other party again. Strictly physical.

As I stated previously, I don't believe true love exist or maybe I just haven't found it. I thought I fell in love with a young lady, she was my first love, although I wasn't hers. We dated for two years, she actually cheated and told me. I would not have had any idea if she wouldn't have said anything. At that time in my life, I was immature, I left her and couldn't forgive her indiscretion. I couldn't fathom the fact that she was with another man. I loved her, she told me the truth that she didn't want to be with any other man. She ended up with her girlfriend. If I knew then what I know now, I would have stayed. As I look back, she was honest about the situation which is rare. I allowed my pride to take over me.

I had to move on, and began to ask myself what factors attracted me to the opposite sex? I came to the conclusion that I am a physical being and I like the body of a woman, her breast and her face.

When I see that certain look that I'm attracted to I just know. I don't have a size preference. I'm attracted to the slim model type as well as the plus size model type. And honestly, I can't see a personality, their inner most being or their character traits. I see what's on the outside. Then look to see if they have the other characters to go along with what I visually see.

At the end of the day, these are truly my views. PJ's philosophy on love. If you are the type of person that believes in love and wants to find true love, I pray you stay that way as long as you can. I wish you well and hope that the love relationship trip does right by you.

DESIRES

THOUGHT NUGGET

Mark 11:24

(New International Version)

> Therefore I tell you, whatever you ask for in prayer, believe that you have received it, and it will be yours.

Bible Commentary:

11:24 Jesus our example for prayer prayed, "Everything is possible for you . . . Yet not what I will, but what you will"(14:36). Our prayers are often motivated by our own interests and desires. We like to hear that we can have anything. But Jesus prayed with God's interests in mind. When we pray, we should express our desires, but want his will above ours. Check yourself to see if your prayers focus on your interests' or Gods.

Throughout the interview with PJ, he concentrated on his sexual desires. While God cares for every area of our lives, he wants his desires for us, and not our own. Hurt and pain can cause us to lose focus of what is really important. There is nothing more important or greater than God's love. It reminds me of lyrics and one of my favorite songs by Fred Hammond, "No Greater Love". If you never heard it before, take the time to listen. The lyrics are below:

> There is no greater love, no greater love
> Than the one You have for me, Lord
> There is no greater love, no greater love
> Than the one You have for me
>
> Your mercy, so tender
> Erasing my transgressions
> There is none greater
> There is none greater
>
> Your mercy, so tender
> Erasing my transgressions
> There is none greater

There is no greater love, no greater love

Than the one You have for me

There is no greater love, no greater love

Than the one You have for me, Lord

Your mercy, so tender

Erasing my transgressions

There is none greater

There is none greater

Your mercy, so tender

Erasing my transgressions

There is none greater

There is no greater love, no greater love

Than the one You have for me, Lord

There is no greater love, no greater love

No greater love

Your love for me is forever

Your love for me is forever

To me there is none greater

To me there is none greater

Your love for me is forever

Your love for me is forever

No greater, no greater

No greater, no greater

Your love for me is forever

Your love for me is forever

To me there is none greater

To me there is none greater

Your love for me is forever

Your love, there is none greater

No greater, no greater

No greater, no greater

Your love for me is forever

Your love for me is forever

To me there is none greater

To me there is none greater

Your love for me is forever

Your love for me is forever

No greater, no greater

No greater, no greater

Your love for me is forever

Your love for me is forever

To me there is none greater

To me there is none greater

Your love for me is forever

Your love, there is none greater

No greater, no greater

No greater, no greater

Your mercy, so tender

Erasing my transgressions

There is none greater

There is none greater

Your mercy, so tender

Erasing my transgressions

There is none greater

Your desire should be God's desire for you. There is no greater Love, then God.

FORGIVE

Gabriel Serafin is a forty-five year old Insurance Agent, married with four children, two adult children and two under the age of eighteen. Gabriel is in a biracial marriage and believes love is unconditional; transcends nationalities, age groups, economic status, and color. Love is when two people care for each other despite the worlds odds. It's that agape love, no matter the faults, mishaps, mistakes, ill-spoken words or actions, you forgive and still love.

I feel I know when I'm in love when being around that person gives me goose bumps, states Gabriel. When you are not in their presence, you have a desire to hear their voice, to smell and caress them, and to see them. You can't stop thinking about them. You contemplate making love to them.

Now, I repeat myself, making love to them, not having sex with them. Making love and having sex are two very different things. You have sex without feeling just satisfying your flesh. When making love you have a spiritual connection with that person, not only emotionally but physically as well, and the two of you become one. Most men and women want to satisfy self without any attachment and move on to the next. As a younger man, I also committed the same acts with no commitment.

Over the years I have grown to know Jesus as my personal savior. Since that time, religion and my relationship with God has helped me to understand what love is. The world's way of love is nowhere close to God's explanation of love. The bible explains what love really is. Until you read the word of God, you have no idea what love is all about. Only in the past two years have I gotten a deeper revelation of Love. People say they are in love with a person, but is the other person in love with you. I believe you can love someone, yet that person is not the right person for you. You have to pray and ask God if it is the right person for you. You will get an inner witness that the person is the one. If you do not end up in marriage that was not the right person. God's word does not return void. His answers are yes or no. So if your fiancé or your boyfriend has not married you and time has passed, you should consult God to make sure this is the right person for you.

Before I got married, I was in a relationship where the women did everything any man would have wanted. She washed my feet, gave pedicures, manicures, prepared home cooked meals, and kept the house tidy. I wasn't mature enough to appreciate those things. It ended up being a bad break up. She left and emptied out my home. That's when I understood the phrase "a woman scorned". I say that, to reiterate, while she was truly in love with me. The feelings were not the same. We both did not know the Lord. We were not right for each other. It was not God's plan for my life or hers. I forgave her for what she had done, I know it was simply out of hurt. But I also had to forgive myself for overlooking a really good woman. But God sent my wife, who completes me and I am very appreciative.

I appreciate my wife enough to know that the act of infidelity is not worth losing her. Men who cheat are greedy and selfish. They don't consider their partner or their family if children are involved. Women tend to believe a man when he says, things are not working out at home and I just need someone to talk to. The talking then leads to sexual activity. Or he tells the woman, that he is in a bad situation and is contemplating leaving his spouse. Of course the woman hangs around with moments of time spent, and he normally does not leave the spouse. If he leaves the spouse and cheated on her, what will he do to you? The woman is setting herself up for hurt. While I say women, this can also happen to a man. Women and men should love themselves enough to not want to share anyone. If a woman or man is married, it should be an automatic off limits.

The love I expect to receive and give is one that is selfless, forgiving and looks out for each other's well-being. I have found that love in my wife and more importantly in God.

FORGIVE

THOUGHT NUGGET

Ephesians 4:32

(New International Version)

> [32]Be kind and compassionate to one another, forgiving each other, just as Christ God forgave you.

Are you holding a grudge, bitterness or anger toward anyone in your past? Past relationship, friendship, marriage or family. Let go of any ill feeling and forgive, in order for God to forgive you. When you forgive others it releases you to receive love. Let go of all the past hurts, pains, disappointments, mistreatment, abuse, and anything that affected your life in a negative manner.

Matthew 6:14-15

(New International Version)

[14]For if you forgive men when they sin against you, your heavenly Father will also forgive you. [15]But if you do not forgive men their sins, your Father will not forgive your sins.

SUCCESS

Today, men are searching for the physical attributes of a woman. Men are looking for the biggest backside, biggest breast, etc. They don't realize that after time passes and she grows older, those attributes won't last forever. What happens when several years later her beauty fades, she doesn't have voluptuous assets anymore and all that is left is personality? Can you still look at her the same way you did when she was twenty and in her prime? Is there still a spark when you see each other; do you still get butterflies in your stomach as well? These are the questions that men should ask themselves when courting a woman. This is where the foundation of love starts, says Derrick Cash, Jr. a twenty-one year old entrepreneur and dog trainer. Derrick is single, but engaged to be married.

Derrick continues, love in my view is companionship, finding someone who meshes with your life, socially, mentally, physically and sexually. Love is giving your whole self to another person. I am currently in love with a beautiful woman, both inside and out. I feel she is my soul mate. She is the ying to my yang. What I lack, she possesses and vice versa. I couldn't imagine loving another person. I hear people state that they are confused because they are in love with two people. That is hard for me to understand. If you truly love one person, you would be loyal to that person and no one else would matter. That's not love what they feel. That's just fleshly desire. Fleshly desire is simply sex. Sex is an important part of love, but sex should not be the foundation for love. Sex outside of marriage is acceptable to people, but not acceptable in Gods eyes. Society has misrepresented sex and love, confusing the two.

I knew when I was in love when I felt a sense of trust, I wanted to satisfy the other person in every way possible. You place that person' goals and dreams as a priority, because you want to see them succeed. I believe God sends you that one true person that you are supposed to be with. You will know. Religion and God play in important role in love. I believe God is love. I also believe that the male should pursue the woman. I am not a Bible scholar, but somewhere in the word it says "he that finds a wife, finds favor in the sight of God and Man". It doesn't say, she that pursues, she that looks for, she that chases on the internet, or she that stalks. No it says "he that finds". When a woman is the chaser, it comes across as desperation on the woman's behalf. I'm a little old fashioned in this area, and prefer to be the hunter.

In a past relationship I was the pursuer and thought that I was in love. I based love on what was lust. Eventually I learned to love her but by that time my relationship was not built on trust and respect, but was based on sex. So, of course that did not work out. It never does. When there is no respect or trust; men and women have a tendency to become unfaithful. There is no particular reason why men do not remain faithful—they just want to see what's on the other side of the fence. It looks great, looks like gold, glitters, or whatever the man's deepest desires are. But at the end of the day it's not worth it. Because all that glitters isn't gold.

If you truly love a person you should want to be fully committed, eventually marrying that person. It should not matter the economic status or social status of the person. While it should not matter to you whether her economic status is good or bad, it also should not bother you if she is more economically stable than you. I don't mind if a woman makes more money than me, I appreciate a progressive woman. I also like a women who has a sense of humor, intelligent, who I can have a conversation with almost about anything, and who desires friendship before a relationship.

SUCCESS

THOUGHT NUGGET

Proverbs 16:3

(New International Version)

> ³Commit to the lord all that you do, and your plans
> will succeed.

Bible Commentary:

16:3 There are different ways to fail to commit whatever
we do to the Lord. Some people commit their work only
superficially. They say the project is done for the Lord, but
in reality they are doing it for themselves. Others give God
temporary control of their interest, only to take control
back the moment things stop going the way they expect.
Still others commit a task fully to the Lord, but put forth
no effort themselves, and then they wonder why they do
not succeed. We must maintain a delicate balance: trusting
God as if everything depended on him, while working as if
everything depended on us. Think of a specific effort that

you are involved right now. Have you committed it to the Lord?

In all areas of our lives we should commit our concerns including success over to the Lord. That includes a successful relationship. I personally believe "Anything worth having is worth working for". Anything worth having is also worth waiting for on God's time table. In the book of Genesis the 29th Chapter, Jacob desired to marry Rachel, through trickery he ended up marrying the oldest daughter Leah, as in those times it was the custom for the eldest daughter to marry first. He worked seven years for Laban (Rachel's father) as a dowry for his daughter Rachel. After he was tricked into marrying Leah, he still agreed to work seven additional years for Rachel.

Although, he did not have to wait that long in order to marry Rachel. Jacob new true success in relationships and life come from hard work and patience. Are you willing to work at your relationship? Are you willing to wait on God's instructions concerning your love life? Do you choose God's success or mans' version of success?

REFRESH

Most women like to go out and go dancing. If you can dance there are women who will like you above other men. Dancing tells a lot about a person. Have you ever been in a night club or event and you see women dancing with each other? That's because most men can't dance. The man who can dance is usually the one who will catch the eye of the prospect says Tony Fryer, Director of Youth Sports—Development and Personal Trainer to professional athletes. Tony is a dedicated father and divorcee.

Tony feels dancing is sexy, energizing and a turn on if done appropriately. I love to dance and it has given me a heads up on opponents in the relationship arena. If you can move your body on the floor then, well you get it. Sex is important in a love relationship or any relationship. But more important is being true to oneself and living in harmony with everyone else. Love is a bond and life together. That bond is sometimes broken but can also last.

I don't have a preference of what type of woman I will dance with or date. Nationality, size, height does not matter. I meet a lot of women who are very bold and persistent in approaching men. This however is not a turn off for me. I have a personal preference for intelligent women, one who I can have a decent conversation with and who is versatile in what we talk about. From world history to the arts. Love for me is broad; I love my family, I love women, I love sports, and I love what I do.

REFRESH

THOUGHT NUGGET

Proverbs 11:24-25

(NIV)

> [24]One man gives freely, yet gains even more;
>
> Another withholds unduly, but comes to poverty.

> [25]A generous man will prosper;
>
> He who refreshes others will himself be refreshed.

Bible Commentary:

11:24,25

... The world says to hold on to as much as possible, but God blesses those who give freely of their possessions, time and energy ....

Tony Fryer is truly a refresher and a motivator. I have witnessed young men and women come up under his tutelage and leave with a new found self-esteem, confidence, and sport know how. He has mentored some of the greats. He gives freely of his time, himself and knowledge. When giving so much out sometimes you need refreshing yourself. Have you given of yourself to anyone lately, not expecting anything in return? In order to receive, you must also give. This applies in love as well. If you love someone you should freely want to give of your time, your energy and yourself.

ABSTAIN

Dr. Larry T. Walthour is a Pastor and Dr. of Divinity, divorced with one lovely daughter. Dr. Walthour has definitely experienced love, although it did not last. He has no regrets and would marry again if the right person came in his life. Dr. Walthour states: I believe in following the biblical principles pertaining to love and receiving a wife.

As a single Pastor, I meet quite a few women. Some women are very forward even the saints of God. Christian women, I am now referring to. They say they pray if the man of God is their husband or not, and God tells them that he is, yet the man of God hasn't heard a word from the Lord. That blows my mind. God is not going to tell one, without telling the other. They both will know, sometimes not at the same time. But eventually, both would get confirmation. I prefer a subtle woman, who is humble and somewhat soft spoken. I like a well dresser, as I like to dress myself. Physical appearance is important.

How you present yourself, is how you feel about yourself. That pertains to men and women alike. "Above all, clothe yourself with love, which binds everything together in perfect harmony." (Col. 3:14) I believe living in harmony requires that we recognize the inherent worth and value of others.

Where division prevail, love and harmony must persist. God's love produces harmony, unity, and liberty in the world around us. While I like for a women to dress well, I should also see qualities of God's love in her. Is she walking in harmony and unity with others? What is her conversation like?

These are important attributes for me. It is important also that a woman is not promiscuous. Although I haven't seen anywhere in the word of God, where you have to remain abstinent until marriage, and if so, I will just lose one crown. I'm joking. It's important to follow God's principles on sex, love and marriage which the foundation is laid out in the word of God (the Bible). I enjoy cultural events as well, so I would prefer a woman who is well cultured and would not mind partaking in other things outside of church.

As long as it is good clean fun, it's not a sin. God wants us to have a balanced life. To give time to him and also enjoy the world and things in the world that God created. I like a progressive woman, not overbearing, but knows what she wants out of life. Able to think for herself and not easily persuaded. As I have not found "that one" yet. I am patient to wait on God until his right timing to marry again. While basking in God's love, he eventually will send me a woman's love.

ABSTAIN

THOUGHT NUGGET

1 Peter 2:11

> [11]Dear friends I urge you, as aliens and strangers in
> the world, to abstain from sinful desires.

Dr. Walthour joked about the state of abstinence and losing a crown. God clearly states that his desire for us is to be free from sin. As we our alien and strangers in this world, our real home is in heaven with our Father. But while in the world we are urged to abstain from sinful desires. That's temptation, sex, immorality, drunkenness and anything that is not of God. We should recognize Gods truth and his way of life. There is no compromising when it comes to God's word. Yes, you should abstain from sex until marriage and any other sinful desire. I don't want to lose a crown or a jewel. What about you?

CONCLUSION:

LOVE "A MANS PERSPECTIVE"

When you say I love you, do you really mean what you say, or is it just something to say to pass time? Are you saying it to get what you want; physically or emotionally? After hearing the perspectives of the men in this book and seeing God's perspective, I pray you can give yourself an honest answer as to what your perspective is on love.

I have observed men that are close to me and those through association. I am under the impression the four letter word "LOVE" has taken on a new definition. Based on my observations, men are asking women—"what do they have to offer financially". "Do you have a home, business, or car"? Women, I am not telling you it is not important for financial stability. I do not want to date based on my financial portfolio. I'm also not saying date blindly, not knowing each other's baggage, which we all have. What I am saying is, these should not be the only criteria for marriage or love. Biblically, when Joseph married Mary, he was a carpenter, the bread winner, the provider and the protector and husband of what would be the most important mother of all times. Mary was a housewife and mother to Jesus. Someone is saying right now, alright, how long ago was that, time has changed. Yes, time has changed, but the word of God remains the same.

I have witnessed several forms of love:

Love that tells no time, has no boundaries, and spreads wide as the sea.

True love does not see faults, does not blame and learns to forgive.

Blind love sees nothing but love itself.

Self-love does not learn to release love to another.

Unselfish love can love without expecting anything in return.

Material love cares only about what one can give or receive in material possessions.

Timeless love is mature and endures all things, the flavor gets better and better over time.

Seamless love has no meaning, no purpose and no plan.

Merciful love is when you're willing to die for another, give your life and shed your blood.

That's the love of Jesus.

I pray you will review the scriptures and read for yourself what God says about love.

INVITATION

Selfless love—a love that gives passes it's desire. A love that sees beyond Selfishness. A love not tainted by society's definition. A love that loves through illness, deformation, helplessness, hopelessness and misconceptions. Have you witnessed this kind of love? When a spouse can no longer take care of themselves and the other spouse loves beyond the circumstances. A dying husband or wife, the spouse still loves until death truly do they part. This is a rarity. Love.

As we each have our own perspective of what we feel love is or should be; how we feel we should receive and give love; God also has a perspective on what love is toward us, the church, and all mankind. Someone reading this book may not know Jesus as his or her personal savior; God wants to pour his love on you. You don't have to wait for a man or a woman to give you the love you feel you need. God wants to give you a love that is everlasting, constant, fruitful and true. If you need this type of love as I do, repeat after me: God I need your love, a love that is forgiving, merciful and true. Come into my life, and I except you as my first love. I denounce the things of my past and except your son Jesus as Lord of my life. Thank you for your love. If you said this and meant it from your heart; you now have an everlasting love with the Father, the Son, and the Holy Ghost. Find a Bible based church so you may grow in the things of the Lord. God loves you so much. I pray this book was a blessing to you.

If you have any comments, please contact Tina Cash on "*Facebook*".

SCRIPTURE READINGS

PASSION	1 Corinthians 7:9
	Proverbs 8:17
AMBITION	Philippians 2:1
	Proverbs 17:17
CREATE	Isaiah 45:7-8
	1 Cor. 13:3-7
PROTECT	Psalm 59:9
	Galatians 5:22-23
SUSTAIN	Song of Solomon 2
LEAD	Exodus 15:13
	Proverbs 31:10-31
PROVIDER	Matthew 6:11-13
DERSIRES	Mark 11:24

	Mark 14:36
FORGIVE	Ephesians 4:32
	Matthew 6:14
SUCCESS	Proverbs 16:3
	Genesis 29
REFRESH	Proverbs 11:24-25
ABSTAIN	1 Peter 2:11

ABOUT THE AUTHOR

TINA CASH is an author, motivational speaker and mother of three sons Derrick Jr., Devon and Dontre Cash. Tina Cash has held several women's conferences and is the founder of Pamper Me Jesus seminars. Ms. Cash aspires to touch the lives of many women and men to enlighten them that there is a better way and a better day through Jesus Christ. With over fifteen years in the ministry, God has given Tina Cash the gift to motivate others to walk into their Divine Destiny.

www.ingramcontent.com/pod-product-compliance
Lightning Source LLC
Chambersburg PA
CBHW030347290526
45785CB00004B/1638